THE TRUE COST OF FOOD

KATIE DICKER

HOW TO SHOP TO CHANGE THE WORLD

First published in 2013 by Wayland
Copyright © Wayland 2013

Wayland
338 Euston Road
London NW1 3BH

Wayland Australia
Level 17/207 Kent Street
Sydney, NSW 2000

Produced for Wayland by Calcium
Design concept by Lisa Peacock

Picture acknowledgements
Dreamstime: Boonsom 26, FabioConcetta 17, Rivertracks 10, Sapsiwai 15, Vicspacewalker
12; EveryChild: Kallappa Mang/MASS 22; Shutterstock: AVAVA 40t, Dmitry Berkut 40b,
branislavpudar 24, M. Cornelius 41, deniss09 39, elwynn 9tr, 25t, Terrance Emerson 2, 7b,
Gena73 31, Joe Gough 36, haak78 8b, 42, Jorg Hackemann 23, JM Travel Photography 44,
kamnuan 11b, LiteChoices 11t, MAC1 27b, Troy Marcy Photography 29b, marco mayer 7t, Stephen
Mcsweeny 8m, 28, michaeljung 8t, 37t, Monkey Business Images 4, 13, 45r, Juriah Mosin 27t, M
R 19t, Korolevskaya Nataliya 21t, OMMB 29t, Wendy Perry 35, Picsfive 19b, 25b, paul Prescott
43, Pressmaster 33b, 45l, Rtimages 34t, Weldon Schloneger 38, smereka 9b, 30, Kailash K
Soni 20, tarasov 37b, Richard Thornton 18, Toa55 34b, Lee Yiu Tung 9tl, 14, Tupungato 21b,
Vibrant Image Studio 5, Watchtheworld 32, Gautier Willaume 33t, zmkstudio 6.; Wikipedia:
Shiny Things 16l.

A catalogue record for this book is available from the British Library.

ISBN: 978 0 7502 7713 6
Printed in China

Wayland is a division of Hachette Children's Books,
an Hachette UK company.
www.hachette.co.uk

CONTENTS

GROWING GREED

Today, the food we eat is grown and produced in every corner of the globe. Our mouths are filled with food from each continent, from European potatoes and Central American pineapples to African cocoa, Asian corn and Australian sugarcane. However, our rich and varied diet comes at a price.

Feed the world

In the developed world, we've come to expect a cheap and plentiful food supply. People have grown used to eating what they want, when they want. And as each generation improves its standard of living, dietary tastes become more sophisticated than ever before.

With a world population already standing at 7 billion, food production is big business. In the UK in 2010, for example, **consumers** spent £182 billion on food. And the demand keeps growing. Despite economic uncertainty, food is a basic requirement for survival, and there are more and more mouths to feed. Food producers and distributors know that playing a major role in the food industry is a sure way to make a **profit**.

Today, supermarket shelves are filled with products that are grown and produced all around the world.

A global industry

Every day, lorries, ships, trains and planes carry goods across continents. In 2010, for example, over 50% of the UK's food came from overseas. The globalisation of trade has provided useful employment opportunities for people in developing countries. Employment levels in the Windward Isles, for example, are closely linked to the international market for bananas (see page 43). But when global economic conditions favour the West, developing countries are caught in a vicious cycle. They need to keep a foothold in the global marketplace, but it's a struggle to make a profit when market prices are so low.

Vulnerable workforce

The demand for food keeps growing and companies are constantly chasing profits. In some farms and factories in the developing world, workers are exploited to keep up with the demand for cheap food. They work long hours for very little pay, often in dreadful conditions. For some workers, a job means a wage and a chance of survival. However, there's little hope of a life outside work. Employees put up with appalling conditions because they have no choice, or they see no way out. Some may be frightened of a jobless future, others afraid of an abusive employer. In the West, workers have a voice and a chance to fight for their rights. But in many developing nations, parts of the workforce have become invisible.

Draining resources

In the Western world, there are costs to human health, too. A rise in cheap, processed food has caused an **obesity** epidemic, and healthcare services are struggling to cope. The natural environment is also suffering. Producing and transporting our food is putting a serious strain on the Earth's resources, and waste products are polluting our planet.

Transportation allows goods to travel across continents, but it has an impact on the environment, too.

5

Supply chain

The food industry is governed by a complex supply chain. And in recent decades, developments in transport, technology and communications have lengthened the process. Products grown in one country may now be processed in another, packaged elsewhere still, and then sold worldwide. As demand grows for particular products, they become more expensive. If the supply is increased, the price falls again. When companies are looking to raise their profits, making larger quantities of cost-effective food is their main goal. They may use cheap labour from workers in the developing world with few, if any, rights to help them achieve this.

The modern world

Although famine and starvation are a terrible reality for many people in the developing world, other countries have never had it so good. In the 1960s, average households in the West spent about a third of their income on food. Now, the figure is less than **15%** (**6%** in the USA). Enhanced production has kept prices low. But the future may tell a different story: drought and **climate change** are having a devastating effect on crop harvests; energy costs are rising; populations are growing; and as parts of the developing world become richer, people's eating habits are changing. If we're unable to sustain a steady supply of food, rising prices could be crippling.

Today, around 50% of pineapples grown in the developing world are exported to other countries.

Since the early 1980s, world coffee consumption has increased by 1-2% a year.

Corrosive culture

As we grow and make more and more food, the Earth's resources are being exhausted, polluted and changed forever. And lives are being made a misery. So what are we, as consumers, to do? As we reach for a snack bar, or ponder our next meal, is there action we can take to make a difference? How does the money in our pockets contribute to our food culture and can we change it? Can we as individuals use our spending power to help break the cycle of excessive food production? In this book, we'll look at how, together, we can work to change the lives of exploited workers, to sustain the world's valuable food resources, and to promote a healthy diet that's also safe for our planet.

Most of the world's corn is produced in the USA, but will climate change affect the production of this important crop?

SHOP TO CHANGE THE WORLD

When you go food shopping, do you check to see where your produce comes from? Are any of the fruit and vegetables grown in your own country? Do you know when these foods are in season? How much food do you buy from abroad?

7

FOOD WORLD MAP

The food industry has become a global phenomenon. In the past 30 years, the value of global exports and imports has risen from around US$1.3 trillion to US$16 trillion.

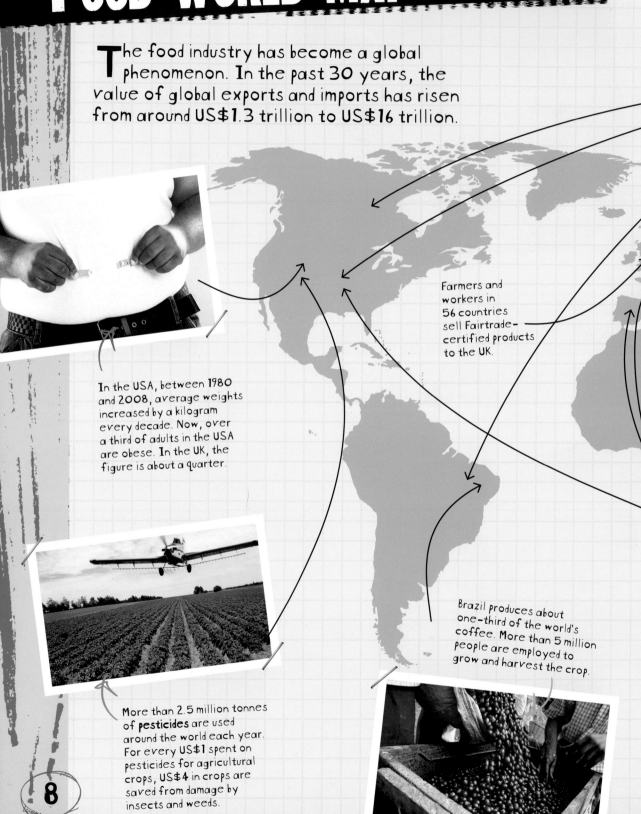

Farmers and workers in 56 countries sell Fairtrade-certified products to the UK.

In the USA, between 1980 and 2008, average weights increased by a kilogram every decade. Now, over a third of adults in the USA are obese. In the UK, the figure is about a quarter.

Brazil produces about one-third of the world's coffee. More than 5 million people are employed to grow and harvest the crop.

More than 2.5 million tonnes of **pesticides** are used around the world each year. For every US$1 spent on pesticides for agricultural crops, US$4 in crops are saved from damage by insects and weeds.

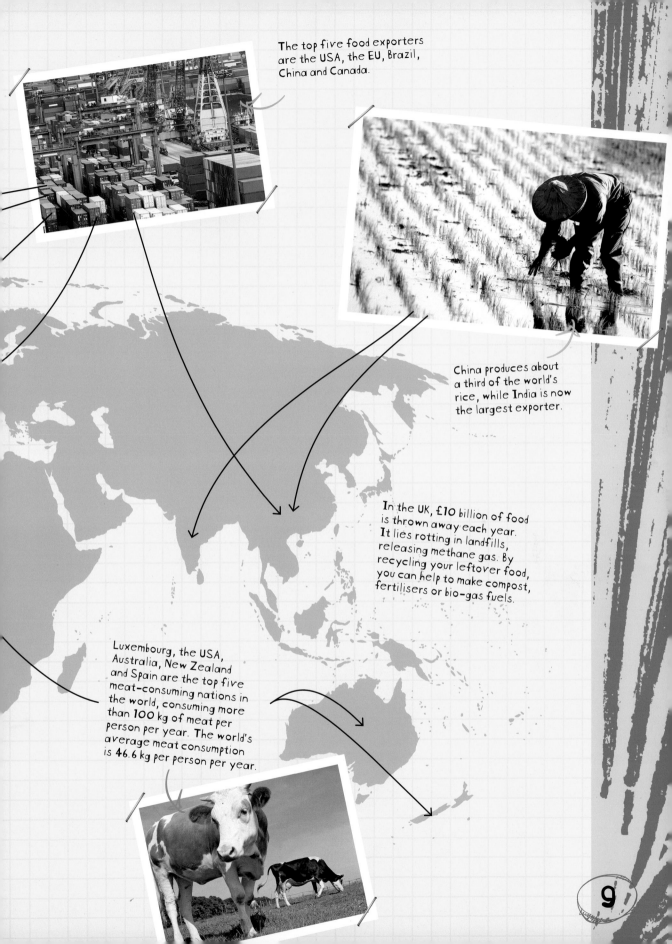

The top five food exporters are the USA, the EU, Brazil, China and Canada.

China produces about a third of the world's rice, while India is now the largest exporter.

In the UK, £10 billion of food is thrown away each year. It lies rotting in landfills, releasing methane gas. By recycling your leftover food, you can help to make compost, fertilisers or bio-gas fuels.

Luxembourg, the USA, Australia, New Zealand and Spain are the top five meat-consuming nations in the world, consuming more than 100 kg of meat per person per year. The world's average meat consumption is 46.6 kg per person per year.

CHAPTER 1

MEETING DEMANDS

As people around the world have worked to improve their standard of living, rapid changes have evolved. Transport has made trade much easier, machinery and chemicals have increased food production, and preservation techniques allow food to be stored for longer than ever before. We've become used to a rich and varied diet. But is this progress **sustainable**?

Cheap labour

Our world population could reach 9 billion by 2050 and this increase comes at a time when the world faces uncertain economic conditions and a changing climate. With an unstable economy, supermarkets are competing to keep costs down for their customers. They want - and need - to stay in business. But they also want to maximise their profits.

Some manufacturers in the developed world choose cheap labour abroad to cut costs. Many countries in the developing world have undemocratic forms of government. They may have more relaxed environmental laws, too. It is easy for companies to use their workforce because employees have no legal rights or chance to complain about their conditions. A **trade union** is something they can only read (or dream) about. And there are few laws to protect against low wages, child labour, poor health and safety standards, and even slavery.

Playing along

But whilst the Western world exploits this cheap labour market, developing nations are playing their own part in the process. They are keen to progress and have their own aspirations. Farms and factories have provided useful employment opportunities for people eager to improve their standard of living, and for countries keen to get ahead. Many employees in Central and South America, Asia, and some parts of Europe, have been exploited to keep up with the pace of progress. As ugly as it may be, forced labour is one way for these nations to get a foothold in the world market.

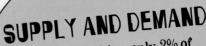

SUPPLY AND DEMAND

In Tanzania, Africa, only 2% of workers are supported by a trade union. This compares to 28% in the UK and 12% in the USA.

Our demands for sugarcane are met by many developing countries, such as Brazil and India.

Cheap food relies on agricultural workers in China and other developing countries.

CONSUMER NATION

China recently raised its economic status by increasing production. China now grows about one-third of the world's rice, for example, and produces 80% of the world's wheat gluten (for bread, biscuits and cakes). Although some workers have been exploited, they have helped to improve the country's fortunes. But at what cost? It is impossible for workers to endure long hours, with little pay and poor conditions, forever. Is exploitation the only way for developing nations to join the Western world? Can we do more to encourage fair economic progress for developing nations? What do you think?

MAJOR PLAYERS

The world's food industry is powered by a huge and complex supply chain. At the top, a small number of global companies support a handful of major supermarket chains. At the bottom, thousands of farmers and their employees work as hard as they can to remain part of the chain.

Concentration of power

Our global food system is like an hourglass: farmers from around the world sell their produce to millions of consumers through a small number of food production companies and retailers. And in recent years, big companies have merged, making them more powerful than ever before.

A tea picker in India makes just 1p for every £1.60 box of tea bags sold in a UK supermarket.

SUPPLY AND DEMAND

When you pay for your food, you contribute towards the cost of growing or making the item, packaging it, transporting it and advertising it. But who makes the most money? When you buy a jar of coffee, for example, about 10% goes to the grower, 10% to the exporter, 55% to the shipper and roaster, and 25% to the retailer.

A vicious circle

Today, major players in the food industry control many aspects of production, from the seeds farmers use to grow their crops, to the fertilisers and machinery they use to tend and harvest their produce. They have a firm grip on the retail side, too, from processing and packaging to transporting and advertising. Above all, they have the power to control prices. They want to maximise profits by keeping costs low. And this is where farmers in developing countries are caught in a vicious circle. They need the work to make a living, but to keep the cost of their goods competitive, they don't get a fair price for their produce.

Keeping contracts

When farmers and factory owners are put under pressure to fulfil large orders and to meet last-minute deadlines, they do what they can to keep up. Initially, they may increase their supply of cheap, manual labour to help meet demands. But if the pressure mounts, they may resort to **unethical** conditions as a desperate measure. Workers' pay may be cut or working hours increased. If the company doesn't meet the terms of its contract, it will risk losing the work to another supplier.

How often do you check where the food you buy in a supermarket comes from and how it was grown or made?

CONSUMER NATION

Are major companies to blame for our food culture? Have a look at the arguments below. Whose side are you on? Is there a way of distributing global food wealth more fairly?

Pros
Supermarkets and food production companies should keep a closer eye on where their goods come from and how they are made. Supermarket policies encourage an unethical culture. 'Buy one, get one free' deals tempt customers by cutting costs and encourage shoppers to look for other good-value products.

Cons
Consumers are sustaining an unethical culture. We've come to rely on a variety of cheap food and we live in a throwaway society. In comparison to shoppers in developing countries, our money gives us the power to make informed consumer choices. Some of the responsibility lies with our purchases.

TRADE RULES

Workers, farmers, companies and multinational corporations all contribute to the food supply chain, but the trading relationship within and between countries also has a significant impact on working conditions. As if mirroring what happens at a local level, rich nations gain an advantage at the expense of the poor.

Tariffs and quotas

When countries trade with each other, governments sometimes add **tariffs** to imports, making them more expensive to buy. These 'taxes' help to raise money for a government. They also give an advantage to items produced locally by making them cheaper than foreign goods. Countries also protect their domestic industries by placing **import quotas** on particular products. By limiting the number of goods that can be imported over a period of time, quotas restrict competition from abroad and encourage products to be made (or grown) 'at home'. And when the price of these goods rises, producers increase their profits.

Free trade

Across the world, there are an increasing number of free trade agreements (FTAs) to promote trade between nations, and encourage investment in a particular region. FTAs can also strengthen relations between nations. Examples include NAFTA (North American Free Trade Agreement) - the largest trade agreement in the world, signed between Canada, Mexico and the USA - which trades goods such as eggs, corn and meat tariff-free.

Agricultural produce accounts for nearly half of world exports of non-manufactured products.

14

Free trade agreements - reducing tariffs, eliminating quotas, and lifting government regulations - make it easier to trade. But they also encourage companies in the West to seek cheap products and cost-effective labour abroad.

The subsidy system

In Europe and the USA, **subsidies** are used to protect the food industry. They allow farmers in these developed countries to sell goods at low prices without losing profit themselves. Problems arise when too much produce (such as sugar or milk) is made and the excess is sold cheaply on the world market. This practice, called 'dumping', forces prices down and farmers in developing nations can't compete.

The effect of subsidies can help to provide cheap food for people in developing countries, but it also means farmers working outside the subsidy system are at a disadvantage. Wealthier nations can afford to subsidise their farmers, but this means developing nations are left behind.

Sugar is an important export for many developing nations, but low prices are forcing farmers out of business.

CONSUMER NATION

Do free trade agreements help to reduce poverty? Take a look at the arguments below. What do you think? How can we trade more fairly to help developing nations prosper?

Pros

Countries won't get rich without being able to trade with each other.

By encouraging exports, free trade agreements open up new markets for developing nations. This can help to sustain economic growth.

Cons

Free trade agreements pass more power to multinational corporations, who can exploit a cheap workforce.

Developing countries compete to attract foreign investors, at the expense of workers' rights.

Small farmers find it impossible to compete.

GLOBAL ACTION

After World War **II**, the global community worked together to rebuild nations following the devastating effects of the war. Countries hoped that a new financial system, with good trading practices, would prevent a repeat of the **Great Depression** that ravaged the economy of many countries and contributed towards the onset of world conflict.

New institutions

As part of this post-war initiative, the International Monetary Fund (IMF) and the World Bank were created. The IMF's role was to stabilise financial markets and exchange rates, while the World Bank would provide investment for reconstruction and development. Today, these institutions still work to promote international trade, to reduce poverty and to sustain economic growth. Some countries contribute money to these institutions, while others are given loans.

In recent years, however, these organisations have been accused by **pressure groups** of ignoring the environmental and social impact of the projects they support, and have been criticised for causing more debt in developing nations. They were set up to promote free trade, but critics argue they are making matters worse.

The World Bank was founded to reduce poverty in developing nations. Its headquarters are in Washington, D.C., USA.

The International Monetary Fund was created in 1944. It aims to improve the economies of member countries.

A struggling nation

For the Caribbean country of Haiti, for example, rice has always been a staple food product. In 1980, Haiti grew all the rice it needed to feed its citizens. But in 1986, in response to a badly needed loan from the IMF, Haiti agreed to relax tariffs on its imports. Now, the country imports 80% of its rice from the USA because subsidised rice from American farmers is cheaper than Haiti's own harvests.

As rice farmers struggled to make a living, it became more tempting to use cheap labour. Some farmers gave up and moved to the cities, but work was hard to come by. Today, the situation is graver still. Haiti suffered a devastating earthquake in 2010 and businesses across the country were destroyed. As the country tries to rebuild itself, there is an ever-greater demand for cheap labour, with the most vulnerable at risk of exploitation.

The destruction caused by Haiti's earthquake in 2010 has left people more vulnerable than ever before.

World referee

Many people look to international organisations to intervene and encourage fair trade. The World Trade Organisation (WTO) was set up in 1995 to promote free trade and economic growth. More than 150 member countries trade according to WTO rules and the organisation works to resolve trade disputes.

But the WTO has been criticised for being a 'rich-man's' club that fails to benefit free and fair trade. In 2003, the WTO's conference in Cancun, Mexico, collapsed because rich and poor nations couldn't agree. Rich countries focused on new trade issues, while poor nations wanted to resolve the effect of subsidies. The conference's collapse was one of the first times developing nations made their voices heard.

SUPPLY AND DEMAND

On the streets of Cancun in 2003, WTO protestors were also having their say – sometimes with devastating consequences. South Korean farmer Lee Kyung-Hae took his own life in protest at US subsidised rice, which was forcing farmers like himself out of business.

17

CHAPTER 2

WORKING LIFE

The workers who supply produce for our supermarket shelves may be happy to have employment. They may need to support a young family or elderly relatives. But as campaigners point out, for some, wages and working conditions are far from fair. And workers may be putting their health – or even their lives – at risk.

Reality bites

According to a report by campaigning group Consumers International, some workers on pineapple plantations in Costa Rica earn the equivalent of about £57 a week. This is £8 above their national minimum wage, but when workers have to do 80 hours a week to earn this basic salary, there's little time left for a life outside work. And when it comes to a 'living wage' - that adequately covers food, shelter, transport, clothing, healthcare and education - it doesn't even meet half of the estimated £137 a week required.

Across the globe, there are similar stories. Many workers are denied employment benefits, such as sick leave, **maternity leave** and overtime payments. Some workers are children deprived of an education. Others are harassed, intimidated or physically abused.

Desperate measures?

Why is the situation so bad? Campaigners say greedy employers increase their production and reduce **overheads** to raise profits. But sometimes, farmers resort to these methods in desperation. When they don't earn enough to cover the cost of running their farm, they may resort to forced labour and dangerous working conditions. Many companies use contract workers, who aren't entitled to benefits and are therefore cheaper to hire. These workers rarely complain because there are plenty of employees waiting to replace them. In food production, the seasonal nature of work encourages employees to increase their hours during peak harvest time, putting their safety at risk.

These children are planting rice in India. Child labour saves employers a lot of money.

Workers in meat-packing factories are often faced with cramped conditions.

CONSUMER NATION

In an ideal world, companies would always work in an ethical manner, treating their workers fairly and making sure that all parts of the food chain are properly managed. But with a vast supply chain, it can be difficult to constantly keep track of where produce comes from. Companies may sub-contract business to factories which they don't own or manage themselves.

Local governments and law enforcement agencies could help to monitor working practices, and consumers could also question what they are buying. Can media pressure and public awareness also encourage a sense of collective responsibility? What do you think?

19

THE WORKFORCE

Across the globe, vulnerable workers are paying the price of other people's greed. Attracted by the prospect of work, but unprotected by government or trade union support, they find themselves caught in a terrible trap. They may be desperate to earn a living – but at what cost to themselves?

Wage attraction

In the developing world, poor workers (often women and children) are attracted by the promise of work and opportunities to earn a wage. Children tend to work for lower wages and are less likely to complain about poor working conditions. Many children work to help their parents - they simply work instead of going to school.

Some governments in the developing world have a different attitude to human rights and labour issues. In many countries, for example, childhood is seen as a time for learning a trade and child labour is culturally acceptable.

These children are lucky to have an education. In some parts of the developing world, children have to work instead of going to school.

Western workers

In the developed world, too, immigrants are drawn to the food industry because they can make more money than they would at home. They put up with poor conditions and dangerous jobs because they're desperate to make a living. Sometimes, these workers are illegal immigrants with limited language skills. They don't even have a voice to defend themselves.

At harvest time, immigrant workers often find temporary jobs in the food industry, but the pay is poor.

No way out

But perhaps the most sinister situation of all is the practice of **human trafficking**, when people are taken against their will as a form of cheap labour. In 2011, for example, the US Equal Employment Opportunity Commission (EEOC) filed a lawsuit after it discovered US farmers trafficking workers from Thailand. Encouraged by the prospect of high wages and temporary visas, the workers had their passports taken away when they got to the USA and were afraid to complain in case they were **deported**. They were then faced with poor pay, rat-infested housing and physical abuse. To make matters worse, they were forced to pay large sums of money to their employer as a 'recruitment fee', putting them in severe debt, from which they could never recover.

With the seasonal nature of food production, many workers are brought in to lend a hand. Arriving illegally, it's almost impossible for the authorities to track them down, and to monitor their welfare. This invisible workforce is one of the most vulnerable of all.

SHOP TO CHANGE THE WORLD

Human rights groups argue that to stop exploited labour you need to raise living standards and education so that workers are empowered to find better jobs. Buying ethical products and campaigning against exploitation by companies, employers and governments, is one way that consumers can help to protect vulnerable workers and to help them make a fair and safe living.

Despite strict immigration controls, some workers still cross borders illegally.

CASE STUDY I
AMIT: MY STORY

Around the world, many children and adults have been forced to work in appalling conditions to support the food industry. Some have no choice. Others are simply working to survive. But whatever the reason, their lives are made a misery. Here, we learn of Amit's story.

Working to survive

Amit lives in South West India. When he was six years old, his father died from malaria. Amit's mother, Shobna, was left to care for her two sons and life was very hard. After two years of constant struggle, Shobna was desperate to provide for her children. She eventually took one of her sons to work with her as an agricultural labourer, and soon afterwards, Amit became a bonded labourer on a farm, two kilometres from their home.

Ten-year-old Amit with his mother, Shobna.

Payment promise

Amit had to live and work on the farm with his landlord, who was a complete stranger. Bonded labourers are often tricked and trapped into working for little (or no) pay, seven days a week. They are promised a lump sum payment at the end of their contract, rather than working for a salary or to repay a loan. From 7 a.m. to 7 p.m., eight-year -old Amit shepherded sheep, cleaned their pens, and fed and protected them. He even had to trek alongside the flock for miles, to try to find them decent food. For all his hard graft, Amit's family was promised two lambs a year (each worth about £33).

Amit worked on a sheep farm, like this one, in South West India.

Far from home

Two other men helped the landlord to manage the farm, but their workload was minimal. It was up to Amit to do most of the work, helping his landlord to make a profit from the sheep and lambs sold for meat and wool. Every night, Amit slept in the pen, protecting the sheep from predators. He was given three meals a day, but when the landlord was on holiday, Amit was left to starve. If he did something wrong, the landlord would shout and scream at him.

After a year, Amit did not receive two lambs. Instead, his mother was given 2,000 rupees (£28), which just about covered her health and household expenses. Amit longed to go home. He wanted to live with his family and to return to school. But for the 18 months that he lived and worked on the farm, Amit was kept captive and only saw his family twice.

A change of fortune

Luckily for Amit, an international development charity called MASS found him on the farm and intervened. They provided counselling for Shobna and support for Amit. Following their intervention, Amit left the farm, returned home and went back to school.

Although Amit is still in education, he's unable to enjoy his childhood to the full. He feels compelled to take leave from school to go and work in a hotel for 50 rupees (56p) a day to support his family. Amit says, "If I go to school, my home cannot run. But sometimes I feel that in spite of these problems, I should go to school."

With thanks to MASS/EveryChild for this case study. To find out more about EveryChild's work with vulnerable children visit www.everychild.org.uk.

LIVING ON THE EDGE

The plight of exploited workers in the food industry is often described as poor pay and conditions. This is the short-term effect of their employment, but there are deeper issues affecting their future. The work can bring a whole host of dangers – from day-to-day hazards to the threat of long-term illness.

A dangerous job

Employees in the food industry face many dangers, regardless of their country of origin. In the West, companies are legally required to carry out health and safety checks to keep their staff safe. But even the most vigilant employers witness accidents from time to time. Wet surfaces or poorly stacked boxes pose risks. Ladders, platforms and crates can cause falls, and workers can put their back and muscles at risk lifting heavy boxes, pushing large loads, or carrying out repetitive tasks. In food processing plants, hand tools and sharp knives have to be used with care. Machinery should be operated correctly, following strict rules, with protective guards and safety switches.

Safety inspectors monitor conditions in food factories to keep staff safe.

Harvesting rice is backbreaking work, and long hours add to the discomfort.

These employees have been provided with overalls and gloves to wear, but in some food processing factories, workers are offered no such protection.

Daily hazards

But consider the plight of more vulnerable workers who face many of these dangers without the support of safety guidelines or protective clothing. Workers in the fields are exposed to dangerous pesticides and **toxic** chemicals without the use of goggles, gloves or masks. Workers in busy packing plants may have no access to a fire exit.

Long working hours put the human body under strain, and when repetitive tasks and cramped conditions are included, it comes as no surprise that workers complain of muscular injuries such as **tendonitis**. Poor lighting can put workers' eyes under strain, and intimidation or abuse can lead to workplace stress.

SUPPLY AND DEMAND

In the UK between 2000 and 2010, there were 77,000 injuries and 36 fatalities in the food and drink manufacturing industries. Each year, nearly 5% of the workforce suffers from illnesses attributed to work in the industry. Statistics in the developing world often go unrecorded, but campaigners argue that if health and safety measures are lacking, the figures are likely to be huge.

25

CASE STUDY 2

DANGEROUS LIVES

The dangers faced by food industry workers often hit the headlines. Each story is as shocking as the last. But despite public outcry and the work of health and safety agencies, the statistics keep coming. And when an invisible workforce is at the centre of the drama, it's almost impossible to ensure these people's safety.

Tragedy in the bay

In February 2004, disaster struck in the beautiful sweep of Morecambe Bay in Lancashire, UK. As evening fell, a group of about 30 Chinese workers were busy collecting cockles at low tide. Unaware of the danger looming (because they couldn't read the tide warning signs on the beach), they gathered handful after handful of cockles. Suddenly one of the workers looked up and saw they were trapped by the fast-flowing tide, with the water lapping in faster and faster. One worker dialled 999 on his mobile phone, but with his poor English, the operator could only hear 'sinking water' before he was cut off. In desperation to stay afloat, some workers struggled to take off their clothes in the dark, icy waters. Many couldn't swim. Twenty men and three women, aged 18 to 45, died in the disaster.

Cockle pickers can face many dangers, such as fast and rising tides.

Hopes dashed

A massive rescue operation tried to save the cocklers, but most were dead before the lifeboats arrived. The workers were illegal immigrants reported to be earning up to £30 a day (when, and if, they were paid). With the modernisation of China, many had lost their agricultural jobs back home and hoped for a better deal abroad. Some had taken out a loan of £15,000 to travel to the UK, expecting to earn more in a month than they could in a year at home. But with no legal work permit, they were forced to take dangerous jobs. The disaster left their children, parents and family members devastated and deeply in debt.

The cockle pickers were reported to be earning £5 for every 25-kg bag of cockles they collected.

Finding justice

The workers were employed by a 29-year-old **gangmaster** who drove his workers to and from the sands and rented them overcrowded accommodation in the surrounding area. Using false cockle picking permits, he employed up to 70 Chinese illegal immigrants. He never collected cockles himself, but sold the shellfish for £20 a bag, taking most of the profits.

The gangmaster was caught and sentenced to 14 years in prison, and his girlfriend and cousin were also convicted. He told survivors to blame the tragedy on two of their dead colleagues, and pretended to be an innocent hired driver. But some refused and testified against him, despite being threatened for giving evidence. The public outcry that followed led to a new Gangmasters Licensing Authority helping to identify migrant workers and to protect them from danger.

A sea rescue operation, in progress. Despite such an attempted rescue, 23 cockle pickers died that day.

3

THE EARTH IN CRISIS

We depend on our planet for the food we eat: meat from animals; leaves and fruit from plants; and water from the rain that we harvest. We need to take care of our planet to protect this essential food supply. But the Earth's health is already under threat.

Sowing and reaping

Long ago, farmers sowed seeds in the autumn to reap a harvest in summer. They waited for the Sun and rain to help their crops grow. Farmers worked with nature to get the best out of the land. But today, in an effort to produce a regular supply of cheap food, fertilisers, pesticides and intensive farming techniques have replaced traditional farming methods.

Fertilisers and pesticides

When fields are farmed intensively, the soil loses its natural supply of nutrients. Farmers use fertilisers to keep the soil rich enough for plants to grow. Natural fertilisers, such as manure and compost, have been used for centuries. But in recent years, chemical fertilisers have become big business. Farmers also use pesticides to protect their crops from weeds, insects and disease.

Fertilisers and pesticides greatly increase the world's food production, but their overuse can be deeply damaging. The chemicals they contain drain into water courses, polluting the environment and posing a danger to human and animal health. When pesticides are used to kill bugs, they harm other creatures, too. They may damage organisms that keep the soil healthy, and kill natural predators or important food sources for other creatures. This can cause the number of plant and animal species to become severely unbalanced, upsetting the natural food chain.

Ladybirds are natural aphid-predators, but pesticides are causing them harm.

Intensive farming

Intensive farming techniques affect the balance of nature, too. Farmers now plant fewer varieties of crops in favour of high-yield products. Crops are also bred to be a similar shape and size, and to have a longer shelf life. On some farms, livestock are kept in cramped conditions and force-fed so that they grow more quickly. Livestock are bred for quality, too. These changes are causing a rapid decline in the diversity of plant and animal life.

SUPPLY AND DEMAND

In recent years, the number of honeybees in the UK and other parts of the world has dropped dramatically. Bees pollinate many important crops, such as apples, and their decline could have a devastating impact on our food supplies. Scientists think the bees may have been damaged by pesticides used on food crops. If the findings are correct, the chemicals we use to protect our crops may actually be causing their collapse.

If honeybee populations continue to decline, fruit crops will be badly affected.

DEVASTATING DEMAND

As the world population grows and farming techniques become more intensive, the Earth's resources are under threat. The next 50 years is set to bring 30% more mouths to feed and the current situation is unsustainable – the more we eat, the more our food sources become exhausted.

Lost land

With the mechanisation of farming methods, food production has increased at the expense of the land. Soil has become less fertile and forests have been cleared to make room for crops and pasture. Scientists estimate that we lose 20,000 hectares of forest per day - an area twice the size of Paris.

Precious water

Our water sources are also under threat. Around 70% of the water we use is needed for farming. This figure increases to 90% in some developing countries, where farmers take ground water faster than it can be replaced, with dramatic consequences. In some areas, for example, rivers used for irrigation no longer reach the sea.

In the USA, eight times as much land is used as pasture for farm animals to graze than it is to grow food directly for humans.

Ocean life

Although intensive farming is managing to maintain a steady supply of livestock, our 'wild' food is seriously in danger. A century ago, there were at least six times more fish in our oceans. We are catching more fish than nature can replace, and many species are on the verge of extinction. Over 90% of large predatory fish, such as cod and tuna, for example, have already been caught.

Fossil fuels

Other precious resources are also in decline. The fuels we need to move machinery, irrigate our land, make fertilisers, power factories, and transport and store our food products are running out. As oil prices inevitably rise, the cost of our food is going to escalate.

Waste products

Waste products from the food industry are also a cause for concern. Every year a cow, for example, releases up to 120 kg of methane in its manure. This **greenhouse gas** traps 23 times more heat in the atmosphere as the same amount of carbon dioxide. According to the United Nations, **18%** of **global warming** emissions come from raising animals for food - more than the world's total transport industry. With meat consumption expected to rise as developing nations adopt a more Western diet, the Earth's climate is under serious threat.

In the USA, more than 40 billion burgers are eaten each year. A quarter-pound of beef takes 1,700 litres of water to produce – to grow the grain to feed the cows.

SHOP TO CHANGE THE WORLD

Where does your food come from? How is it produced? How much do you throw away? Around 7.2 million tonnes (£12 billion worth) of food and drink is thrown away by households in the UK every year, wasting the energy, water and packaging used to produce, transport and store it. By throwing away less food, we can help to save valuable resources and reduce greenhouse gas emissions. Buying local produce is also a good way to save the fossil fuels used to transport it.

SUPPLY AND DEMAND

- It takes about 3,000 litres of water to produce one kilogram of rice.
- In the USA, 19% of the nation's fossil fuel consumption is used for the food industry – more than any other sector of the economy.
- Around five square metres of rainforest is cleared for grazing land for every pound of beef produced, releasing about 225 kilograms of carbon dioxide in the process.

CASE STUDY 3
THE PRICE OF PINEAPPLES

Three quarters of the pineapples sold in Europe now come from Costa Rica. Consumers in the West have been enjoying this tropical fruit at knockdown prices, but the real cost falls on plantation workers and families living close by. As the industry expands, Costa Rica's natural environment is also paying the price.

Rapid expansion

Pineapples are now one of Costa Rica's main exports. In just ten years, the land used to grow pineapples has expanded by around 300%. **Deforestation** (often illegal) to make way for pineapple plantations is having a devastating effect on the region. The soil is full of chemicals and losing its fertility. In the rush to develop the industry, important regulations have also been overlooked, damaging both the environment and human health.

As forests are cleared to make way for pineapple plantations, the landscape in Costa Rica is changing.

Demanding work

For the plantation workers, unrealistic production quotas and falling prices bring long hours of backbreaking work in the hot Sun (for reduced pay). Julio gets up at 4 a.m. to go to work on a pineapple plantation. He used to walk, but he saved up for several months to buy a bike. Now the journey takes him half an hour. When he gets there, the long working hours are terribly uncomfortable. In the fields, he works in the hot Sun (or heavy rains) with no shelter. The work is demanding and repetitive - planting seedlings, weeding crops and picking fruit.

Cocktail of chemicals

Pineapples need large amounts of pesticides to grow, with regular and very intensive treatment. Without proper regulations in place, these chemicals have been polluting rivers and streams. Fish are dying and water supplies are becoming contaminated. Workers are exposed to a cocktail of chemicals, and complain of headaches, sickness, allergies, skin diseases, respiratory problems and more serious conditions.

Alba lives next to the plantations. Her water has been polluted by chemicals, including a pesticide linked to cancer. "We asked the government to do an analysis of our water," she says, "It was contaminated by 22 types of chemical." For three years, the community has had to rely on tanks of clean water supplied by the government. "Sometimes we go for four days without water. I now have many chronic illnesses - loss of vision, pain in my joints, damaged lungs, and many infections. Five years ago I was a healthy woman with no problems with illnesses. Now every day my health is deteriorating."

Pesticides used to grow pineapples put farm workers' health at risk.

Supermarkets in the West may sell pineapples cheaply, but what impact does the low price have on the workers who grow them?

Alternative methods

In other parts of the country, pineapple farmers are trying to grow their crops in a more sustainable way. With the help of Fairtrade subsidies (see page 42), they can afford to use alternative methods. Instead of filling the soil with fertilisers, they keep it rich with compost. But with pineapple prices falling, and international companies competing for a place on the supermarket shelf, the demand for Fairtrade pineapples is under serious threat.

Case study source: Consumers International (www.consumersinternational.org). Names have been changed.

SUPPLY AND DEMAND

Costa Rica's pineapple exports grew from US$142 million in 2001 to US$484.5 million in 2007, and exports have continued rising by up to 12% each year. Between 1999 and 2006, the USA and Europe doubled its imports of Costa Rican pineapples. The USA now imports 90% of its pineapples from Costa Rica.

4

YOU ARE WHAT YOU EAT?

Intensive farming methods bring a plentiful supply of fresh food to our table, but there are hidden health hazards. Polluted air and water, contaminated food and the use of artificial chemicals can all take a toll on our wellbeing. We may be well fed, but our health is at risk.

A chemical diet

More than 2.5 million tonnes of pesticides are used around the world each year. In the West, exposure is usually too small to pose a serious risk. But in some developing countries, poor safety standards on farms are putting lives at risk. The farms' workers and families living close by are the worst affected, but consumers can also be at risk. Governments place strict guidelines on pesticide residues left on our food, but in some nations, standards are poor. Many countries are trying to reduce their use of pesticides and to follow stricter guidelines.

Crops are sprayed with chemicals for maximum production, but at what risk to our health?

Fighting infection

With intensive farming practices, animals live in cramped conditions where disease can quickly spread. To keep their livestock healthy, farmers give animals **antibiotics** in their feed. In the USA, for example, it is estimated that **70%** of antibiotics sold are used in the farming industry. Instead of treating sick animals, the medicines are used to prevent infection. This overuse of antibiotics is causing resistant strains of bacteria to grow. And there have been reports of resistant bacteria being passed to humans in the food chain, putting our health at risk of more untreatable infections. Governments are now working to put tougher regulations in place, and to find alternative solutions such as improved hygiene, vaccinations and breeding livestock to resist infection.

Factory chickens are kept in cramped conditions that put them at risk of injury and infection.

SUPPLY AND DEMAND

Processed food uses additives, preservatives, flavourings and colourings to make our dishes tastier, more attractive, and less likely to go rotten. Some of these use natural ingredients while others contain artificial chemicals. Although strictly regulated, campaigners argue their effects on our health are uncertain. There have been reports of allergies in some people, and a suspected link between additives and hyperactivity in children. Our growing appetite for convenience food could be putting our health at risk.

Unbalancing nature

Many animals are also given hormone supplements in their feed to encourage growth, boost milk production and help breeding. There are concerns that traces of hormones in meat and milk could be harmful to our health. Scientists are also concerned about the environmental impact. If cow manure contaminates nearby water sources, for example, hormone residues can harm plant and animal life.

Food supplements are added to grain to keep cattle healthy and to maximise milk and meat production.

DISASTROUS DIETS

With access to a cheap and plentiful food supply, consumers in the West (and those adopting Western eating habits) have never had it so good. But waistlines are expanding. Inactive lifestyles combined with a fast food culture, are causing record levels of obesity. And the resulting health costs are escalating.

Common causes

Obesity occurs when a person eats far more calories than their body can burn. Around 500 million adults worldwide are now obese, and another billion are overweight. As food becomes cheaper and more varied, people are encouraged to eat more. Marketing and advertising campaigns promote processed food, and our busy, stressed lives fuel bad eating habits. Instead of walking or cycling, many people use cars or public transport. And the development of technology has changed the nature of manual work and forms of entertainment.

Processed food may be quick and convenient, but it contains high levels of fat, salt and sugar.

A growing problem

Scientists estimate that if trends continue, nearly 60% of the world's population could be overweight or obese by 2030. The world is becoming more urban. In 1900, 10% of the world's population lived in cities. Now the figure is more than 50%. And urban life brings greater access to food and a fast food culture. Free trade has also brought cheaper commodities, and as the developing world becomes richer, Western diets and lifestyles are being adopted around the globe. The demand for meat, for example, is set to rise 25% by 2015.

SUPPLY AND DEMAND

In 1951, a woman's average waist size in the UK was 70 cm. In 2004, this figure had risen to 86 cm. This means that waist sizes, on average, have been increasing by about 3 cm every decade.

Health impacts

People who are overweight are more susceptible to medical conditions, such as heart disease, diabetes, cancer, respiratory diseases and arthritis. Each year in the UK, for example, up to 30,000 people die prematurely from obesity-related conditions. And many more cope each day with the effects of their body size. In the developing world, where there is less access to quality healthcare and information about healthy lifestyles, waist sizes are increasing at an alarming rate. Obesity used to be a problem mainly in the West, but over the past 20 years, China, India and other developing nations have experienced an obesity epidemic.

Financial costs

In the USA, obesity cases have tripled in the past 50 years, with around two-thirds of adults now overweight or obese. This situation has added US$190 billion a year to healthcare costs. But there are other hidden costs, too. Reports estimate that the US pays an extra US$5 billion a year on additional jet fuel to fly heavier passengers and US$4 billion a year on additional fuel for car transportation. Sickness and absence from work is damaging the economy, and health insurance companies have had to raise their premiums for everyone to cover additional medical costs.

Our busy lives encourage a fast food culture. But what price are we paying for modern eating habits?

ALTERNATIVE SOLUTIONS?

Many aspects of the food industry are threatening our environment and putting our health at risk. And with rising populations, the situation is unsustainable. So what does the future hold for our daily diets? Can we find alternative food sources that are safe for our health and our natural surroundings?

Working with nature

Organic food is produced using environmentally and animal friendly farming methods. Farmers keep the soil fertile and healthy by rotating crops, and using natural forms of fertiliser. Animals are reared in spacious surroundings, requiring no antibiotic or hormonal intervention. And any pesticides that are used come from natural sources.

Organic produce is rich in vitamins, minerals and enzymes - the good things we need to keep our bodies healthy - and free from chemicals and artificial additives. Supporters say the taste is better, and there are no hidden fats, salt or sugar. Campaigners point out that it's kinder to livestock, too. Although organic food costs more on the supermarket shelf, the price reflects its methods of production. But with a slower production time, and a limit to seasonal produce, can organic food meet the demands of a rising population?

By restricting the use of artificial chemical fertilisers and pesticides, rearing animals and crops for food organically reduces pollution and greenhouse gas emissions.

38

Science vs. nature

Another alternative - but controversial - food source is genetically modified (GM) food. By genetically altering food in a laboratory, scientists can breed crops that grow quickly, resist disease, and contain additional nutrients. GM wheat, for example, produces chemicals that deter aphids and attract aphid predators such as ladybirds and wasps.

With a rising population increasing the demand for water, energy and food supplies, supporters of GM food say it could be an ideal food source. Almost a billion people in developing countries do not get enough food. And when 30% of food is lost to pests before it can be harvested, GM crops could be a valuable alternative. But its safety for the environment, and for human and animal health, is still in question.

New beginnings

In 1996, scientists in Scotland **cloned** the first mammal, Dolly the sheep. Similar to an identical twin, but born at a different time, cloned animals are genetically identical. Animal cloning can help to improve the quality of livestock, helping farmers to produce copies of their best animals that are then bred to resist disease, and to produce more milk and good quality meat. In the USA, meat and milk from cloned cows, pigs and goats are available to consumers. But in other countries, the debate continues about the safety of cloning and its ethical status.

GM tomatoes last longer, look redder and, some people say, taste better. But critics argue that altering the genetic composition of a tomato goes against the laws of nature.

CONSUMER NATION

Is it right to meddle with the laws of nature to provide food for humans to eat? Have a look at the arguments below. What do you think?

Pros

Cloning disease-resistant plants could help to address the issue of hunger in the developing world, save millions of pounds in farming costs, and reduce the environmental impact of chemical use. Instead of breeding more cattle with no guarantee of the quality of their beef, farmers can reproduce good quality cows. This means less waste and less strain on the Earth's resources.

Cons

There's no certainty that cloning is safe. This new science could expose humans to health risks.
Cloning is an unnatural form of reproduction, and could cause defects or suffering in animals.

5

CAMPAIGNING FOR CHANGE

Around the world, governments, companies, organisations and ordinary people are campaigning to highlight the true cost of the food industry. With new forms of global communication, the work of activists in particular is helping to raise public awareness. But how far do these efforts go? Can they bring lasting changes?

In the spotlight

In the early 1990s, the media turned its attention to the plight of exploited workers around the world. The public outcry and pressure that followed led many major corporations to adopt new codes of conduct. International organisations and pressure groups work to resolve the problem of exploited labour. Environmental groups have also been campaigning about the plight of our planet, and public health agencies have been trying to promote healthy eating habits.

Public demonstrations are one way to raise awareness and to pressure governments and companies to make changes.

Working together

With a long and complex food supply chain, who's to blame for our food culture? What can individuals do to make a difference? Can altering our food habits change things for the better?

In an ideal world, consumers would only buy organic, sustainable and ethical purchases and companies would tailor their products to meet this demand. In the real world, this kind of collaboration is hard to achieve. But individuals can - and should - make a difference.

Taking action

If you want to take part in this process, you can choose to become more informed about your shopping choices. In the supermarket, check food labels for their country of origin. Use customer feedback forms to request ethical products, and contact store managers about their goods. Where possible, support companies with ethical policies. Websites such as Gooshing UK and the Ethical Company Organisation can give you tips and advice (see page 47). You could choose to buy Fairtrade-certified items (see pages 42-43). These may cost a few pence more than other brands, but you would be supporting the people who have worked hard to grow or produce them.

At home, you could encourage your family to avoid wasting food, to buy only what's needed and to try some creative cooking with leftovers. Make compost if you can, and support local food recycling schemes to reduce the amount of food that goes into landfill.

Joining a group

The Internet is full of ideas of groups you could support or join to make a difference. Read about their campaigns and find out if there is anything you can do to help. If you feel strongly about a particular situation, add your voice to the protests. Why not sign a petition, write to the government to complain, or contact your local MP?

Compost is a natural fertiliser made from leftover fruit and vegetable cuttings.

SHOP TO CHANGE THE WORLD

When you buy goods from a supermarket, you are telling the company that you like, need or want what you are buying. This has intensified in recent years, with the use of loyalty cards. Supermarkets can look at customer behaviour and identify what brands and products are popular. Stores respond to customer behaviour to keep shoppers happy and their profits healthy. How many Fairtrade-certified items does your family buy? Your shopping receipts can send a message to the supermarkets. What do they say about your family's shopping habits?

FIGHTING FOR FAIRNESS

In the late 1980s, a new system of trade certification was created in the Netherlands. Now known throughout the world as Fairtrade, the movement seeks to improve working conditions for farmers in developing countries by guaranteeing a minimum price for products and safe working practices, as well as providing investment for local communities.

Early days

Whilst the seeds of Fairtrade were sown in Europe in the 1960s, the idea of certification brought the movement to our supermarket shelves. In the Netherlands, in 1988, Mexican coffee was sold with a certification mark to show consumers that their purchase would improve the lives of coffee farmers. Today, many food products are Fairtrade-certified, including cocoa, coffee, tea, sugar and bananas. The movement is organised by individual groups in different countries, such as the Fairtrade Foundation (in the UK) and Fair Trade USA (in America).

Coffee farmers receive valuable support from Fairtrade. It takes four years for a coffee plant to bear fruit, and another five years to produce a full harvest.

A helping hand

The end of the 1990s saw one of the biggest trade disputes in the food industry, involving a third of WTO member countries. The USA and five South American countries complained to the WTO about EU tariffs used to support banana-growing nations in Africa and the Caribbean. When the WTO forced Europe to change its policies, it had a serious effect on Caribbean farmers. In nations such as the Windward Isles - where bananas provide almost half of the country's exports - the share of the UK banana market fell from 45% (in 1992) to less than 9% (in 2009). The number of banana farmers fell from 27,000 to 4,000 and high unemployment and poverty threatened the island's communities.

Around 100 million tonnes of bananas are consumed every year, of which about 15 million tonnes are exported.

Since 2000, the Fairtrade movement has been helping over 3,000 of the remaining farmers to regain a foothold in the market. Guaranteed a Fairtrade price for their produce, they have been able to build their confidence again. The **Fairtrade premium** has also helped to supply fertilisers, pest and disease control, and to support social, economic and environmental development in the region.

Raising awareness

There's no doubt that Fairtrade campaigns have had an impact on farmers in the developing world. But the movement has also contributed a great deal to raising public awareness in the West. Fairtrade products are more expensive than supermarket-own brands, but they have helped to raise a consumer conscience.

SHOP TO CHANGE THE WORLD

In the UK, the Fairtrade movement has extended to towns, universities, churches and schools. Would you like your school to be a Fairtrade school? Could you help to make it one? Fairtrade schools use Fairtrade tea and coffee in the staffroom and Fairtrade products in cooking classes and in the canteen. Pupils learn about Fairtrade issues and tell others about their campaigns. Find out more from www.fairtrade.org.uk.

SHOP TO CHANGE THE WORLD

There's a worldwide chain of responsibility for a fair, safe and environmentally friendly food industry. As the Fairtrade philosophy goes, 'small actions add up to big changes that make the world fairer for everyone'. Campaigners warn that we can't delay in our fight to improve the future for people and for our planet.

Taking responsibility

Multinational corporations, governments, employers and consumers all play a part in the process. Governments and corporations may have more direct power when it comes to trade practices, but they rely on the support of the people. Without votes or customers, they have no power at all.

If campaigners continue to raise awareness, to protest against unfair practices and to gain support for their projects, important changes are achievable. Campaigns can support food industry workers across the globe, and can encourage the care and protection that's needed for the health of the planet.

A farmer holds rice plants she has harvested in Kampong Cham Province, Cambodia. Campaigns can give support to farmers and other workers in the food industry in their efforts to feed our growing world population.

Time for change

Campaigners aiming to redress unfair imbalance in the food industry say we are all now faced with a choice - we can either continue along the current path or do what we can to allow people, wherever they live and whatever they do, to earn a fair living and to work in safe conditions.

Critics say that companies need to monitor their food supply chains and to denounce the use of forced labour; governments need to tighten their laws to monitor working practices, and to encourage other nations to do the same; and consumers need to make informed decisions about their shopping choices and their eating habits. Developing nations want to improve their status. Some may even want to make their mark on the world stage. But their development should be possible without workers paying the price.

Spreading the word

As global communications develop, the world becomes ever smaller. This makes trade easier than ever before, but it also means people's voices can be heard across continents. Pressure groups are now spreading their messages to more corners of the globe. Campaigners say that a major step towards change is the power of education, because what people know and understand - and do together - makes them stronger. Perhaps with a new generation of smart shoppers we can one day hope for a fair, safe and sustainable diet.

By working together, we can help to make our food supplies sustainable and our planet healthier for future generations.

Ethical shoppers know where their products come from and that the people who produced them worked in safe conditions and were paid a fair wage.

GLOSSARY

antibiotics   medicines used to treat infections caused by bacteria

climate change   changes in the Earth's weather patterns, particularly rising temperatures, over a long period of time

cloned   when scientists make a living thing that is genetically identical to its source

consumers   people who buy products, such as food, for personal use

deforestation   to cut down or clear most trees in a forested area

deported   to be banned from living in a country

Fairtrade premium   a sum of money given to Fairtrade farmers to support the local community

gangmaster   someone who employs large numbers of workers, often illegally and for very little money

global warming   the rise in the average temperature at the Earth's surface

Great Depression   a severe worldwide economic recession that took place in the decade before World War II

greenhouse gas   a gas, such as carbon dioxide or methane, that traps the Sun's heat and causes global warming

human trafficking   when people are transported and forced to work for others, often for little (or no) money

import quotas   limits to the number of goods that can be imported by a country

maternity leave   a period of paid absence from work for a woman to have and care for a baby

obesity   a medical condition where someone is severely overweight

organic food   food produced without the use of artificial chemicals

overheads   the money needed to run a business

pesticides   chemicals used to kill pests, especially insects, that can harm crops

pressure groups   groups that campaign for a particular cause, and try to influence governments, companies or organisations to change their behaviour

profit   the money a business earns after expenses have been subtracted

subsidies   sums of money, usually paid by a government, to help sustain an industry

sustainable   possible to continue, without long-term side effects.

tariffs   taxes added to the cost of imported goods

tendonitis   a medical condition where the tendons (attaching muscles to bones) become inflamed, often because of overuse

toxic   poisonous; harmful to health

trade union   an organisation that protects the interests of workers

unethical   not following acceptable rules or behaviour

FOR MORE INFORMATION

Books

Fair Trade (Explore), Jillian Powell, Wayland, 2012

Fair Trade (Hot Topics), Jill Hunt, Heinemann Library, 2012

Feeding the World (Food and Farming), Richard and Louise Spilsbury, Wayland, 2011

Feeding the World (World at Risk), Anne Rooney, Franklin Watts, 2009

Websites

The Fairtrade Foundation
www.fairtrade.org.uk
Find out more about the work of this UK charity supporting disadvantaged producers in the developing world.

Fairtrade International
www.fairtrade.net
This organisation sets Fairtrade standards and supports Fairtrade producers around the world.

The True Cost of Food
www.truecostoffood.org
Watch this 15-minute educational film about sustainable food.

Ethical Company Organisation
www.ethical-company-organisation.org
This consumer organisation provides clear and comparable ethical information on thousands of companies, for you to make informed consumer choices.

Gooshing UK
www.gooshing.co.uk
This ethical shopping tool helps you find products that are supplied by ethical companies.

INDEX